SALT BABY

DISCARD

SALT BABY

Falen Johnson

Salt Baby
first published 2013 by
Scirocco Drama
An imprint of J. Gordon Shillingford Publishing Inc.
© 2013 Falen Johnson

Scirocco Drama Editor: Glenda MacFarlane
Cover design by Terry Gallagher/Doowah Design Inc.
Printed and bound in Canada on 100% post-consumer recycled paper.

We acknowledge the financial support of the Manitoba Arts Council and The Canada
Council for the Arts for our publishing program.

Library and Archives Canada Cataloguing in Publication

Johnson, Falen, 1982-, author
    Salt baby / Falen Johnson.

A play.
ISBN 978-1-897289-89-1

    I. Title.

PS8619.O4613S24 2013   C812'.6   C2013-901592-2

J. Gordon Shillingford Publishing
P.O. Box 86, RPO Corydon Avenue, Winnipeg, MB Canada R3M 3S3

For Grandma Betty

Nia:wen to my family. You inspire me to no end.

Special thanks go out to Yvette Nolan who was there every step of the way. To Native Earth and the Young Voices program for listening. To Patrick Bramm for your support and understanding when I was being a pain in the ass writer. To Rob and Sean for letting me storyboard on our apartment walls. To Planet IndigenUS, the IMPACT Festival, Fu-GEN, the Ontario Arts Council, and the Next Stage Festival. And to my Grandpa for the words of wisdom. I will keep listening.

Characters

Salt Baby: ....Mid to late twenties. Mixed blood.

Alligator (Al): ....Salt Baby's boyfriend. Mid to late twenties.

Dad: ....Salt Baby's father.

Grandpa: ....Salt Baby's grandfather.

Clara: ....Salt Baby's aunt. Mid sixties.

Doctor: ....A doctor.

Psychic: ....A psychic.

Cheryl: ....Alligator's mother.

Terry: ....Alligator's father.

Wanda B: ....A sales clerk.

Elder: ....An elder.

Philip: ....The most "Indian" man in the world.

TV Host: ....Voice only.

TV Guest Female: ....Voice only.

TV Guest Male: ....Voice only.

Production History

Salt Baby received a workshop production that took place at Theatre Passe Muraille Back Space, Toronto, October 8-17, 2009, with the following cast:

SALT BABY .... Paula Jean Prudat

ALLIGATOR / PHILIP .... James Cade

DAD / TERRY .... Mike Bernier

GRANDPA / CLARA / DOCTOR / PSYCHIC / CHERYL /
WANDA B / ELDER..Michaela Washburn

Directed by Yvette Nolan

Lighting Design by Michelle Ramsay

Costume and Set Design by Jackie Chau

Sound Design by Richard Lee

Stage Manager: Stephanie Nakamura

Falen Johnson

Falen Johnson is Mohawk and Tuscarora from Six Nations. She is an actor, playwright and emerging dramaturg. She is a graduate of George Brown Theatre School. Selected theatre credits include: *The Only Good Indian* with Turtle Gals Performance Ensemble, *The Triple Truth, Savage, Strong Medicine, Death of a Chief, A Very Polite Genocide,* and *Tombs of the Vanishing Indian* all with Native Earth Performing Arts. She has also been seen in *The Ecstasy of Rita Joe,* a co-production between Western Canada Theatre and The National Arts Centre. Falen was seen in *The River* with Nakai Theatre as well as *Tout Comme Elle,* a co-production between Necessary Angel and Luminato. Falen recently performed in *Where the Blood Mixes* with Saskatchewan Native Theatre.

A café or a bar. It is late in the evening. A couple sits in first date position negotiating distance and affection.

ALLIGATOR: Really?

SALT BABY: Yep.

ALLIGATOR: Huh. *(Beat.)* Neat.

SALT BABY: Neat?

ALLIGATOR: Yeah, I don't know. Neat.

SALT BABY: What about you?

ALLIGATOR: Well my mom is Scottish and my dad is English and Irish. So I'm pretty white.

So what else are you? You're not full, right? How much Indian—shit... Sorry. Is that like totally offensive? Uh, Native or...Aboriginal or...any help here would be much appreciated...

SALT BABY: I say Indian but I don't like people to say that until we really know each other, you know? First Nations seems pretty safe to me, but everybody wants to be called something different these days.

ALLIGATOR: OK so how "First Nations" are you? 'Cause you don't really, you know, you don't really look like one, a First Nations.

SALT BABY: Uh, I'm about three quarters.

ALLIGATOR: How does that work?

SALT BABY: Well my mom's half Mohawk. Her Dad was a

Mohawk chief, a hereditary chief. He was married
to a white woman. And my Dad's Tuscarora, full.
So fractions, right? Three quarters. I guess. The
government doesn't really agree with my math.

ALLIGATOR: What do you mean?

SALT BABY: In the opinion of the government if you have one
parent with any white blood it decreases the rest of
your Indian blood. So by their standards I'm half, I
think.

ALLIGATOR: You should find that out. I'd want to.

SALT BABY: I'm Indian enough to get the card right?

ALLIGATOR: Aww! No way! Can I see it?

SALT BABY: Alright but my head looks big.

ALLIGATOR: Even better.

SALT BABY: Screw you.

She hands him the card.

ALLIGATOR: Whoa! Your head is big.

SALT BABY: Told you.

ALLIGATOR: Wait, wait, wait… What's this? Expiry date?

SALT BABY: Yep. I expire. No longer Indian after 2012.

ALLIGATOR: What? That's insane. Hey can we use this here to
pay for our food and stuff?

SALT BABY: Uh no. It doesn't work like that.

ALLIGATOR: No eh? So can you say anything in Mohawk or
Taah-ta- taahs *(He struggles.)* —again a little help
here…

SALT BABY: Tuscarora?

GRANDPA enters. ALLIGATOR is unaware of him. SALT BABY senses him.

ALLIGATOR: Yeah. That one.

SALT BABY: Nothing in Tuscarora, only a few words in Mohawk.

ALLIGATOR: Say something.

SALT BABY: No.

ALLIGATOR: Come on say something in Mohawk. It'll be hot.

SALT BABY: You think it'll be hot eh? *(Beat.)* Alright. Let's see... OK, got it. You ready big boy?

ALLIGATOR: Yes I am.

SALT BABY: *(She is sex.)* When I look at you, all I can think is *gwiss gwiss otah*. (Pronounced gwiss gwiss oh-tah.)

GRANDPA and SALT BABY laugh. ALLIGATOR is turned on.

ALLIGATOR: What does it mean?

GRANDPA: It means pig shit.

SALT BABY: It's a secret.

ALLIGATOR: You know any more?

SALT BABY: I used to. I went to a Mohawk immersion school when I was a kid.

GRANDPA: You used to teach me.

SALT BABY: I used to sit on my Grandpa's lap after school and teach him what I was learning. Those words are the only ones I really remember, the words he quizzed me on.

ALLIGATOR: You wanna sit on my lap and teach me.

SALT BABY: Not really.

ALLIGATOR: Can't blame a guy for trying. Come on, teach me
              something.

SALT BABY: Why?

ALLIGATOR: 'Cause I don't know any other languages. I don't
              know anything about being Scottish or English or
              Irish. It'd be neat.

SALT BABY: Again with the *neat*? What's with you and *neat*?

ALLIGATOR: Come on just teach me something.

SALT BABY: I don't even know if what I know is right anymore,
              so much of it has faded over the years.

ALLIGATOR/
GRANDPA: Just try.

SALT BABY: Alright. Dog is—

SALT BABY/
GRANDPA: *Erhar.* (Pronounced air-o-hall.)

ALLIGATOR: *Erhar.*

SALT BABY: This is stupid.

ALLIGATOR/
GRANDPA: Keep going.

SALT BABY: Star is—

SALT BABY/
GRANDPA: *Otsisto.* (Pronounced o-jis-ta.)

ALLIGATOR: *Otsisto.*

SALT BABY: Cricket is...shit I used to know this one... It's...

GRANDPA: *Taraktarak.* (Pronounced Ji-lick-Ji-lick.)

SALT BABY: *Taraktarak.*

ALLIGATOR: *Taraktarak.*

GRANDPA: You don't know any more?

SALT BABY: I knew more when I was a kid. I don't even know if that was right.

ALLIGATOR: You could learn more if you wanted to couldn't you?

SALT BABY: I just don't know what it is I'm supposed to be learning.

ALLIGATOR: What's wrong with Mohawk?

GRANDPA: So the answer is learn nothing?

SALT BABY: It's just that it's a huge commitment.

GRANDPA: There isn't much time. Not as much as you think.

ALLIGATOR: You should at least try.

SALT BABY: I know.

GRANDPA: Who's the guy?

ALLIGATOR: At least you have some culture; I'm just some white guy.

SALT BABY: Just some white guy.

ALLIGATOR: So you grew up on a Reservation?

SALT BABY: Yeah.

GRANDPA: *(Mocking.)* Reservation.

ALLIGATOR: How far north is it?

SALT BABY: It's actually south of here. Six Nations. You remember that standoff that happened a few years ago? It was all over the news. That's where I'm from. My whole family still lives there.

ALLIGATOR: No way. That's where you're from?

GRANDPA: He's about to ask a bunch of stupid questions isn't he?

SALT BABY: Uh huh. White people are nuts. Sorry. Not you.

ALLIGATOR: No it's true, white people can be nuts, but so can First Nations people. What's with the tire burning?

SALT BABY: Aw shit I dunno. Someone one told me it had something to do with—

SALT BABY /
GRANDPA: Distress. Distress signals.

GRANDPA: I'm getting out of here before this gets ugly. Want a Werthers?

SALT BABY: Yeah.

                       He gives her a candy and exits.

                       I wish they wouldn't do it. It looks bad. I was there at the standoff.

ALLIGATOR: No shit? What was it like?

SALT BABY: It was kinda amazing.

ALLIGATOR: Amazing?

SALT BABY: Well the feeling of being there, you know? The feeling of standing on the highway, this road that I had driven down so many times and then I was standing on it. It felt so strange.

ALLIGATOR: Were people throwing rocks and punching each other out?

SALT BABY: Not when I was there.

ALLIGATOR: Did you wear a bandana and ride around on an ATV?

SALT BABY: You know the news really sensationalized it. Made it look like Armageddon. It wasn't like that. I mean there was some violent stuff that happened, but when I was there it was just kinda quiet on our side. We just stood and listened to them, the white people yelling stupid shit at us. I think most of us just found it kinda hilarious. They were yelling, "We've got Tim Hortons, we've got Tim Hortons." And then they started singing *O Canada*.

ALLIGATOR: *O Canada*? Jesus, that's lame. The stuff I saw on the news was pretty ridiculous, fat white guys yelling, "This is our nine eleven!"

SALT BABY: That was priceless! I went to high school with that guy.

ALLIGATOR: You totally dated didn't you?

SALT BABY: Oh yeah. Totally. He has a monster cock.

ALLIGATOR: Oh you can totally tell.

SALT BABY: Sick.

ALLIGATOR: So…

SALT BABY: So?

ALLIGATOR: What do you wanna do now?

SALT BABY: Well I gotta be up early so I should get home.

ALLIGATOR: Can I walk you?

              She contemplates.

SALT BABY: Sure.

              Transition to…

              SALT BABY and her DAD at home, walking on the Rez.

SALT BABY: The ground in the city feels so hard. Sometimes I walk beside the sidewalk because I think I'm going to forget what grass feels like. People look at me like I'm crazy.

DAD: It's in your blood. Your blood needs to feel the grass and see the stars. It must be hard to not see the stars up there in that big city.

SALT BABY: You think that's true? That my blood needs this? To feel the grass and see the stars? Isn't that buying into that romantic Indian bullshhh... *(She stops herself.)*

DAD: You need to spend more time here, at home with your family. You belong here.

SALT BABY: Maybe I just need better shoes.

DAD: You need money?

SALT BABY: Usually.

DAD: I mean it. You should come home. Get outta that damn city.

SALT BABY: Yeah but at least up there I get wireless Internet and a cell phone signal. Besides what I do if I moved home? Work at the video store? Or a smoke shack? I don't think so.

DAD: Be better than that bar you work at.

SALT BABY: Probably. But I got things going on up there.

DAD: Sounds like a boy.

SALT BABY: Not just him. Other stuff too.

DAD: So there is a boy.

SALT BABY: Yeah, I guess there is.

DAD: Who is he?

SALT BABY:	Just some white guy.
DAD:	Sounds like you really like him.
SALT BABY:	He's funny.
DAD:	If you like him that's all that matters.
SALT BABY:	*(Beat.)* I would like to move back here, just not right now. Someday.
DAD:	Well we got the land. If you want to build on it, it's here for you. Been here for generations.
SALT BABY:	How long has it been in our family?
DAD:	Since I can remember.
SALT BABY:	Do you know who lived here first?
DAD:	I think it was my great-grandfather.
SALT BABY:	And where did he come from, before here?
DAD:	The states I think. Niagara Falls maybe.
SALT BABY:	But you don't know for sure?
DAD:	Well I've always just been from here.
SALT BABY:	And that's enough for you? To just be from here?
DAD:	Yeah it is.
SALT BABY:	Wish I felt that way.
DAD:	Why shouldn't you?
SALT BABY:	'Cause when I walk through the city no one knows that I am, that I am Indian and that's really hard. It makes me wonder why I look the way I do. You know kinda white.
DAD:	'Cause you are kinda white.
SALT BABY:	But how white? What else is in here? I've been

thinking about it a lot lately. What do you know about our family history?

DAD: I'm Tuscarora that's what I know.

SALT BABY: And we know that's on Grandpa's side, but what about the rest of it?

DAD: Could be impossible to know that.

SALT BABY: Because of the lack of paper trail?

DAD: Who was writing them papers out? I don't think the Indian agent really cared what kinda Indian we were as long as we sent our kids to their schools, stayed on the Rez and off the sauce. And there were all those people who switched bands in the twenties.

SALT BABY: Switched bands?

DAD: Back in the twenties a lot bands had really low numbers so people switched to keep the numbers up so that nations wouldn't go extinct.

SALT BABY: Really?

DAD: I guess they felt they had to.

SALT BABY: I'm gonna ask around. Someone's gotta know something.

DAD: Talk to Clara. She knows about that stuff.

SALT BABY: Yeah maybe I will.

The city. SALT BABY and ALLIGATOR sit in the same bar/café as they did on their first date. They are both more at ease with each other. They play a game of 'would you rather.'

SALT BABY: Alright, you ready?

ALLIGATOR: Bring it.

SALT BABY: OK. Klingon or Ferengi?

ALLIGATOR: Aww shit, good one. I'm gonna go Klingon. I couldn't deal with the Ferengi teeth.

SALT BABY: Totally. The teeth it's too much.

ALLIGATOR: OK… Data or Spock?

SALT BABY: Data.

ALLIGATOR: He's a robot.

SALT BABY: He'd probably be good at it then. You now. Deanna Troi or Beverly Crusher?

ALLIGATOR: Crusher for sure. I've never gone ginger. And she's a doctor.

SALT BABY: Yeah but you know her and Picard totally did it so you'd be sloppy seconds.

ALLIGATOR: Whatever, you'd fuck a robot.

SALT BABY: He's "programmed in multiple techniques, a broad variety of pleasuring."

ALLIGATOR: You are such a nerd.

SALT BABY: What?

ALLIGATOR: Alright. Your turn. OK Data, robot fucker, or… RoboCop?

SALT BABY: Easy. Data.

ALLIGATOR: Oh my god you are in love with that robot!

SALT BABY: Think about it. RoboCop had all those emotional problems. Remember how he stalked his wife? Driving by her house all the time. Creepy.

ALLIGATOR: I don't know, I think your love for Data is a little suspect.

SALT BABY: Like you've never thought about banging a robot.

ALLIGATOR: No.

SALT BABY: Liar. Daryl Hannah. *Blade Runner*.

ALLIGATOR: *(He contemplates.)* OK yeah. Still that's Daryl Hannah, not Data.

SALT BABY: Oh whatever.

ALLIGATOR: So did you guys have a good time?

SALT BABY: What?

ALLIGATOR: On the weekend I tried to call you but I guess you were like in deep space with your robot boy toy Data.

SALT BABY: Oh shut up. I was on the Rez. Went home for few days to visit my dad.

ALLIGATOR: How was that?

SALT BABY: He would've liked it if I could have stayed longer.

ALLIGATOR: Ah yes parent guilt. My mom's really good at that, I swear she can cry on cue.

SALT BABY: You get along with your parents?

ALLIGATOR: Yeah, we get along OK.

SALT BABY: Just OK?

ALLIGATOR: We have our shit just like any other family.

SALT BABY: Like?

ALLIGATOR: Just normal family shit.

SALT BABY: Such as?

ALLIGATOR: I don't know, just shit.

SALT BABY: Oh come on! I taught you Mohawk and you can't

even tell me that, oh I don't know, that daddy touched you? *(Beat.)* Oh god, he didn't did he?

ALLIGATOR: *(Beat.)* He did. Daddy touched me.

SALT BABY: Oh god.

ALLIGATOR: I'm kidding, fuck! My dad's a bit of a dick but he never molested me.

SALT BABY: Jesus Christ, you scared the shit out of me.

ALLIGATOR: I don't know if my parents are normal parents. My mom's a bit of a drunk but it's sorta endearing.

SALT BABY: Endearing?

ALLIGATOR: Yeah, she drinks too much chardonnay and dances to Fleetwood Mac. If she drinks enough she gives me money.

SALT BABY: That sounds pretty harmless. Kinda adorable.

ALLIGATOR: Unless you're eight and she's supposed to be picking you up after soccer practice.

SALT BABY: Ooooo…

ALLIGATOR: Yeah. But we get along pretty good now. She was young when she had me, people are idiots when they're young, I get that now.

SALT BABY: And?

ALLIGATOR: And?

SALT BABY: Well we know your dad didn't molest you, but what else?

ALLIGATOR: He's just quiet. He always seems kinda sad like he's thinking about something he's missed or lost or something.

SALT BABY: I think all dads are sorta like that.

ALLIGATOR: Is your dad like that?

SALT BABY: Yeah. He's pretty quiet, so when I get him talking I really try to listen.

ALLIGATOR: And what about your mom?

SALT BABY: She met a white guy after my parents split and now she walks around doing her best to pretend she's white. We don't really talk. I'm just glad I got my dad.

ALLIGATOR: You guys sound pretty close.

SALT BABY: I mean we don't talk all the time and I certainly don't tell him everything, but yeah we talk about stuff.

ALLIGATOR: What kind of stuff?

SALT BABY: The Rez, what's going on down there, who's pissed off at who. When I was home he was telling me some stuff about our family history.

ALLIGATOR: Oh yeah? My mom was all into ancestry dot com for a while. Turns out we are Scottish and English and Irish.

SALT BABY: That is so not fair. If we were white I could Google our last name and find out the name of the boat we came over on, when my great-great-great-grandparents were married, names of family pets.

ALLIGATOR: Oh yeah. It's so easy for us.

SALT BABY: It's easier you can't deny that.

ALLIGATOR: There has to be some record.

SALT BABY: Not really.

ALLIGATOR: Why don't you just get your DNA tested?

SALT BABY: DNA test?

ALLIGATOR: Yeah they're all over the place online. You send them a DNA sample and they tell you your genetic background.

SALT BABY: That seems so…easy.

ALLIGATOR: Nothing wrong with easy.

SALT BABY: You are such a douche.

ALLIGATOR: Just sayin'.

SALT BABY: I guess I could look into it.

ALLIGATOR: Being easy?

SALT BABY: No you dick. The DNA test.

ALLIGATOR: You should. People find out that they have blood from all over the place.

SALT BABY: I don't know if I wanna find that out. Or at least find out like that.

ALLIGATOR: Everyone's just a mish mash of everything anyway, we're all mixed in someway.

SALT BABY: I wish that offered some comfort, all it seems to offer is this sense of impending doom. This inevitable "oneness" that everyone is striving for, everyone except me.

ALLIGATOR: Sounds like a load of hippie bullshit to me.

SALT BABY: I know right!

ALLIGATOR: I'll help you look into it, the DNA stuff, if you want.

SALT BABY: Yeah?

ALLIGATOR: Sure it'd be neat.

SALT BABY: Again with the neat?

ALLIGATOR: You want my help or not?

SALT BABY: Sure sounds neat.

> *A house on the Rez. SALT BABY and CLARA drink tea. There is a plate of Indian cookies that SALT BABY eats with great delight.*

CLARA: Holy! Slow down gwiss.

SALT BABY: Sorry. You can't get these in the city. Thanks so much for this.

CLARA: You know I can give you the recipe. Think your dad has it actually.

SALT BABY: Not just the cookies and tea, but talking to me. Sometimes it's hard to ask family these questions.

CLARA: Well, I don't know that much…

SALT BABY: No, it's good. Anything helps. Really. It's been so hard finding reliable facts. Everybody says different stuff and you never know what's true.

CLARA: It's all part of the oral history.

SALT BABY: I just worry that people get creative with the oral history. So I figured out a way to know everything for sure. I'm gonna get my DNA tested.

CLARA: Noooo! You can't. Why would you want to do that?

SALT BABY: I'm curious. And it's a for sure way to know everything.

CLARA: They're gonna tell you you're Russian or something.

SALT BABY: If I'm Russian then shouldn't I know that? Wouldn't that be as important as being Indian?

CLARA: They're gonna keep you on file.

SALT BABY: I've done some research and some places say they destroy the results after they give them to you.

CLARA: They *say* that. You watch they're gonna clone Indians!

SALT BABY: I'm still thinking about it. I might not.

CLARA: (*Audible breath.*) I wouldn't do it.

SALT BABY: But it's my DNA. Shouldn't I be allowed to do what I want with it?

CLARA: Think about the bigger picture. This is bigger than your questions. This is bigger than you. Think about it seriously, very seriously.

SALT BABY: I will.

CLARA: So who is he?

SALT BABY: Who?

CLARA: The guy. Oh come on, it's all over you. You've got that "getting some glow."

SALT BABY: Oh god!

CLARA: Well?

SALT BABY: Yes there is someone.

CLARA: And?

SALT BABY: It's pretty good. It's actually kinda great.

CLARA: Where's he from?

SALT BABY: The city.

CLARA: White guy?

SALT BABY: Yeah, white guy.

CLARA: Be careful. White guys you know. You'll always be his rebellion, the leather jacket that pisses off his parents, the exotic fruit.

SALT BABY: I don't think he's like that. He gets it. Sort of. He's learning.

CLARA: Don't you ever get tired of teaching them?

SALT BABY: Yeah I do.

CLARA: Well just remember the future is in your womb.

SALT BABY: Then I feel bad for the future.

CLARA: I'm not joking. You have a lot of responsibility.

SALT BABY: I suppose.

                Late at night in ALLIGATOR's apartment. ALLIGATOR and SALT BABY in bed. SALT BABY is wide awake. ALLIGATOR sleeps deeply. GRANDPA enters.

GRANDPA: Well we did side with the Queen but I don't think this is what she had in mind.

SALT BABY: Aw, Jesus I know, I know. But he's not that bad, really.

GRANDPA: Hey you like who you like, I'm not judging.

                SALT BABY gives him an 'Oh really look.'

GRANDPA: What? He looks like a pretty shitty hunter, that's all. It'd disappoint your dad.

SALT BABY: He's really not the hunting type and I don't think I'd send him out into the bush with my dad and guns.

GRANDPA: Probably for the best.

SALT BABY: He's good at other things.

GRANDPA: Like what? Fitting in small spaces?

SALT BABY: Stop. He's really good with computers, that kinda stuff, that's what he does.

GRANDPA: As long as you like him, that's all that matters.

SALT BABY: He wants me to move in with him.

GRANDPA: You haven't been dating that long is that a good idea?

SALT BABY: I like him. It feels right. Plus it'd be cheaper for me.

GRANDPA: You'd be living in sin.

SALT BABY: Oh my god, like you practice any sort of religion.

GRANDPA: Baptist.

SALT BABY: Yeah right.

GRANDPA: It's true.

> *ALLIGATOR stirs.*

GRANDPA: Well at least he isn't a Wop.

SALT BABY: You did not just say that.

GRANDPA: What?

> *SALT BABY laughs and shakes her head. ALLIGATOR wakes.*

ALLIGATOR: What are you laughing at?

SALT BABY: Nothing. Funny dream.

ALLIGATOR: Come here.

> *They embrace. GRANDPA looks away. For the next few lines GRANDPA looks around the room,*

picking things up, putting them down, flipping through books, etc.

So have you thought about it anymore?

SALT BABY: The move-in thing?

He nods.

I mean yeah, of course I want to. I like you and I like this, I just worry, you know. What if it just ruins a good thing?

ALLIGATOR: It's up to you. You're over here every night anyway. I just thought it made sense. But I get it. I don't want to mess up a good thing either. So we can just keep things the way they are and when we're ready we can try it out. If you want. It's cause I snore isn't it?

SALT BABY: Yes. That's it. I just want you to know what it is you are getting into here. I want you to know me before we do this.

ALLIGATOR: OK.

SALT BABY: Yeah? OK?

ALLIGATOR: OK.

They embrace. GRANDPA looks away.

GRANDPA: Aaaah! Quit that!

SALT BABY: Tell you what, if in two months everything is the way it is now, I'm staying here all the time, then—

ALLIGATOR: You'll at least pay some rent?

SALT BABY: *(Looks to GRANDPA.)* I'll move in.

ALLIGATOR: Two months.

SALT BABY: Two months.

The embrace again and GRANDPA exits.

On the Rez again.

SALT BABY: After all this asking around everything just seems more unclear. I've got more questions than I did before. So I was thinking that there is a way to know my background for sure. To know everything.

DAD: Yeah?

SALT BABY: I wanna get my DNA analyzed.

DAD: DNA analyzed? What you gotta do for that?

SALT BABY: There are all these places online, you send them a cheek swab and they analyze it and they send you your genetic make up, everything that's in you in percentages.

DAD: Well don't tell me.

SALT BABY: You're not curious at all?

DAD: That's kinda scary huh?

SALT BABY: That's why I wanna do it.

DAD: What do you think you're going to find?

SALT BABY: I'm not sure.

DAD: And you really wanna know?

SALT BABY: I think so. It could change a lot for me and for you.

DAD: That's why I don't want to know. I know all I need to. I like having status.

SALT BABY: It's not like that really means anything. Status. Lots of full bloods can't even get status. If an Indian woman married a white man she lost her status, if you joined the army, if you wanted to drink, all that Bill C-31 crap.

DAD: Well I'm happy with my card. I like my rights as a card carrying Indian.

SALT BABY: You just like your tax-free trips to Future Shop.

DAD: It's my right.

SALT BABY: So there's this other thing. With the DNA test.

DAD: Yeah.

SALT BABY: Well the test can only track my X chromosome, Mom's side of the family, to be able to track my Y chromosome I'd need a Y donor. A male relative to donate DNA.

DAD: Uh huh.

SALT BABY: So I was wondering if you'd be willing to donate some DNA. It's just a cheek swab, not like a needle or anything.

DAD: Oh I don't know.

SALT BABY: I wouldn't tell. I could just keep it to myself.

DAD: Like you could keep that a secret.

SALT BABY: I could.

                He gives her an 'Oh really look.'

SALT BABY: I could!

DAD: This from the girl who tells everyone what I bought them for Christmas.

SALT BABY: That was forever ago.

DAD: Two years ago.

SALT BABY: I got excited.

DAD: And who told Clara when I hit her dog?

SALT BABY: It slipped out.

DAD: I don't think so. Sorry kid.

SALT BABY: You won't even think about it?

DAD: I don't want to be anything different than what
                I've been my whole life. This land, this place,
                these people, this is me. A pie chart or a graph can
                say what ever it wants about me, but I know who
                I am.

SALT BABY: Yeah.

DAD: You wanna grab some greasy food from the chip
                wagon?

SALT BABY: They still selling bottle rockets?

DAD: You bet.

SALT BABY: OK. Dad?

DAD: Yeah?

SALT BABY: I'm going to find out what one way or another.

DAD: I know.

                He exits. She follows.

                *SALT BABY and ALLIGATOR's apartment. She
                reads from a computer screen.*

SALT BABY: Online past life regression kit. Learn the secrets of
                your past lives from the privacy of your own home.
                Free thirty day trial. Alright, let's try this. Read the
                steps to me.

ALLIGATOR: You realize how fucking stupid this is right? An
                online self-conducted past life test?

SALT BABY: Well its not self-conducted if you're here, right?
                Helping? Come on it's cheaper than a DNA test.

ALLIGATOR: I got a better idea.

                        He paws at her. She pushes him away.

SALT BABY: Come on don't. Please. Just do this for me.

ALLIGATOR: What does it really matter?

SALT BABY: Fuck you! I can get someone else to do this you know? If it's such a big deal to help me out with something that's important to me then I'll just ask someone else.

ALLIGATOR: It says it can take up to forty-five minutes.

SALT BABY: God! Just forget it. You've never been able to do anything for me for forty-five minutes.

ALLIGATOR: Hey! Fine. I'll do it. But it's game over after forty-five minutes.

SALT BABY: Fine sounds about right.

ALLIGATOR: OK. So… *(He reads from the computer.)* Lie down and get comfortable.

                        She lies down.

SALT BABY: OK.

ALLIGATOR: Take your pants off.

SALT BABY: What? *(She sits up.)*

ALLIGATOR: Test says so. You wanna find out about your past lives better take your pants off.

SALT BABY: You are such an ass. Stop!

ALLIGATOR: Alright. Fine. Continuing. Spit on your hand and gently grasp—

SALT BABY: You perv! Seriously?

ALLIGATOR: OK, OK. I'll be good. Real good.

SALT BABY: Don't.

              She lies back down.

ALLIGATOR: Breathe deep and imagine a white orb...*pssht*. Fuck already with the "orb" talk.

SALT BABY: (*Sitting up.*) Are you gonna do this or not?

ALLIGATOR: Alright, alright. Orbs though? Christ.

              She lies down again.

              (*Reading.*) OK so breathe deeply and imagine an orb of light passing over your entire body relaxing you and creating a glow of security around you. (*Beat.*) You close? To being safe that is?

SALT BABY: Yes, I'm good, asshole.

ALLIGATOR: Now envision yourself walking down a set of stairs. At the bottom of the stairs there is a door and beside the door is a couch. If you feel ready walk through the door, if you are not ready sit on the couch and relax until you feel ready. (*Beat.*) Do you feel ready?

SALT BABY: I did until you asked me a question, now I have to sit on the couch.

ALLIGATOR: Shit. (*Beat.*)

SALT BABY: OK go.

ALLIGATOR: Open the door. And through the door is a room. In the room there is a window with the curtains closed and a set of controls. The controls consist of a green button and a red button. The red button takes you back to the safety couch and the green button opens the curtain. Do you see the door?

SALT BABY: Mmmm.

ALLIGATOR: I will take that as a yes. You better not fall asleep on me. OK, when you are ready, push the green button.

SALT BABY is in a doctor's office. DOCTOR enters with a clipboard.

DOCTOR: OK, so I have your results here and what I am seeing is that you in fact belong 100% to the Aboriginal...Native Canadian...uh...First Nations genetic family.

Upon closer inspection I see you have a mix of 50% Mohawk, 25% Cayuga and 25% Tuscarora.

SALT BABY: No way. Cayuga? *(Beat.)* Huh. Sorry it's just a bit of a shock. It's really not what I was expecting. Like at all. Those numbers sound a bit round to me, a little too perfect. That's weird. So that's that then. Well. OK.

DOCTOR: Now as a full-blooded Indian we are going to want to keep track of you. If you'll just give me your right hand I will brand you and you can be on your way.

SALT BABY: What? No way!

DOCTOR: Yes way! I have your results and what I'm seeing here is that you are in fact 76% belonging to the Aboriginal... Native Canadian...uh...First Nations genetic family.

Upon closer inspection what I see is that you are a mix of Irish, Scottish, and French on your Caucasian side and that on your Aboriginal side, you are Ojibwe.

SALT BABY: Irish, Scottish, French and Ojibwe? Does that make me sorta Métis? That doesn't make any sense at all. I grew up in Iroquois country. My GRANDPA was a hereditary Mohawk Chief.

DOCTOR: Science does not lie. Numbers do not lie. You can turn your status card in at the front desk.

SALT BABY: What?

DOCTOR: I said I have your results and what I am seeing here is that you are in fact 100% belonging to the Caucasian genetic family. Congratulations. I'm sure your family will be very proud. Good work. Here are the keys to your new house and a cheque for a thousand dollars! No, just kidding, but seriously, welcome to the club.

SALT BABY: A hundred percent white?

DOCTOR: Upon closer inspection of your results I see that your Caucasian cocktail is made up of English, Dutch, and Spanish. Wow. A colonial cocktail of conquering! That's some pretty powerful blood you got there missy.

SALT BABY: No, no, no. I can't be that. That can't be right. I'll take it again.

DOCTOR: Nope sorry results are final. No do-overs.

DOCTOR exits.

SALT BABY: What? No! Let me see the results. Let me see them! I'll take it again! I'll take it again! I'll take it again!

Shift to SALT BABY and ALLIGATOR's apartment. SALT BABY wakes with a start.

What the—?!

GRANDPA enters.

GRANDPA: Hey, you alright? Bad dream?

SALT BABY: Real bad. The worst.

He sits beside her she rests her head on his shoulder.

GRANDPA: You OK?

SALT BABY: I don't know. I think I am and then I don't.

GRANDPA: You wanna talk about it?

SALT BABY: Not really.

GRANDPA: How about a story?

SALT BABY: Sure.

GRANDPA: OK, let's see...

SALT BABY: Not the one about you playing poker with the devil.

GRANDPA: Alright. There once was this old woman—

SALT BABY: God, not that one, it scares the shit out of me.

GRANDPA: OK fine. This one is about Rez dogs.

SALT BABY: Rez dogs?

GRANDPA: Did you ever wonder why there are so many Rez dogs?

SALT BABY: 'Cause no one gets their dogs fixed on the Rez?

GRANDPA: Nope. You ready to hear the real story of the Rez dogs?

SALT BABY: Sure.

GRANDPA: I only know this because I saw something once, a long time ago, something I wasn't supposed to see but I did.

                One night late, real late, after playing cards in Ohsweken *(Pronounced Oh-sh-wee-ken)*, I was headed back home and heard this sound coming from the ditch, sounded like a wounded dog. So I walked toward the ditch to see what it was. I don't know why, why I would want to see a wounded dog, when you see those things they get burned in your head, never go away those sights. Anyways, I got close to that ditch and sure enough it was a dog. It had been hit by a car. Guts spilling out. Real bad shape this dog was in. I had seen this dog and I couldn't very well just leave it to die slow like that, so I went down in that ditch, lifted my boot over the dogs head and—

SALT BABY: Whoa! This is supposed to make me feel better?

GRANDPA: It gets better, just hold your horses. So I lifted my boot over the dog's head and the damndest thing happened. That dog's head split into two heads and then the body split into two bodies and then two tails until there was two dogs in that ditch with me. You see Rez dogs, they gotta keep going, anyway they can. They've adapted to survive.

SALT BABY: That's gross and funny at the same time. Thank you.

GRANDPA: No problem. *(He begins to exit.)*

SALT BABY: There are some things I wish I could ask you.

GRANDPA: There are others to ask. Ask. The longer you wait the further away the answers get.

              A PSYCHIC's house. Crystals and cards, beads and incense, the sound of a TV (cartoons) somewhere in the distance.

SALT BABY: Hello? Hello?

PSYCHIC: *(From offstage.)* Alright dear. I'll be out in one sec. Just make yourself comfortable. *(To her children.).*Rain!

Get off of your sister! Serenity, I will give you something to cry about! *(She enters.)* Hello dear. Alright. Have a seat. *(She breathes deeply.)* May I see your hand?

SALT BABY: Sure.

PSYCHIC: Close your eyes. *(Beat.)* Mmm hmm. OK, so I receive a lot through Native American teaching and the first thing I get when I sit with you is the armadillo. Armadillo medicine to the Native Americans is all about boundaries. Set boundaries and remember that earth is about honouring your truth, so set boundaries according to what your truth is. Also for you I see the eagle. Eagle medicine is all about solo flight, going on your own. Are you leaving a relationship now?

SALT BABY: Uh no.

PSYCHIC: No? Are you leaving your job?

SALT BABY: Nope.

PSYCHIC: I also get the black panther for you. The black panther to the Native people is all about going into the unknown. Don't be afraid of the unknown. Alright, so what would you like to ask?

SALT BABY: Well, I was wondering who you see around me in terms of ancestors.

PSYCHIC: Alright sure. Hmm… Yeah. OK. So you were and actress in France in the 1400's, and you also had a past life in South Africa. Are you going to Australia?

SALT BABY: Not that I'm aware of.

PSYCHIC: 'Cause I get that around you. I also get the name Rose. Is there a Rose on your mother's side?

SALT BABY: On my father's side.

PSYCHIC: Yeah, she's by you. Also the name Marie...or Mary. So you definitely get Rose as someone who's by you. Anything else?

SALT BABY: No, I guess not. *(She takes out some money.)* Can you make change?

PSYCHIC: Sure just give me one second.

                PSYCHIC takes money and exits.

                SALT BABY and ALLIGATOR's apartment.

ALLIGATOR: I don't get it. I mean would it be so bad if you found out that you're like, one quarter Native? Would that be so bad?

SALT BABY: Yes it would be that bad. It would.

ALLIGATOR: Why? I don't get it. You'd still be you.

SALT BABY: No, I wouldn't be me. I would feel like I had been living a lie. It would feel like my entire existence was bullshit. It's different for Indians.

ALLIGATOR: It's always different for Indians.

SALT BABY: Well it is. Your people tried to exterminate us, colonized us.

ALLIGATOR: My people?!

SALT BABY: Not your people exactly.

ALLIGATOR: I didn't have shit to do with colonization.

SALT BABY: Look the point is I have always been this, my family has always been this, and to be anything else or mostly anything else would not only affect me but them too. My family has been living through the aftermath of genocide, residential schools. You wanna tell my dad, whoops! There's been a mistake, looks like you didn't have to go to that awful school. Here have your culture back.

ALLIGATOR:　You don't need to be so sensitive. Just calm down.

SALT BABY:　Oh my god. Fuck yourself. You couldn't understand what this feels like.

ALLIGATOR:　You're right. I could never understand what it feels like to define myself by someone else's standards.

SALT BABY:　This isn't about that. It's bigger than that.

ALLIGATOR:　You're racist.

SALT BABY:　Jesus fuck.

ALLIGATOR:　You are.

SALT BABY:　Explain.

ALLIGATOR:　You think you need to look like an Indian from fucking *Dances with Wolves*. You buy into it. You're your own worst enemy. You blame everyone else but it's you, it's all you.

SALT BABY:　Say whatever you want but you can't understand this, this un-belonging. I've been told I look white for my entire life. I can't remember not knowing it. When I was born they called me Salt Baby. One look at me and that's what people said.

ALLIGATOR:　Aren't you ever happy about it?

SALT BABY:　Happy about what?

ALLIGATOR:　That you don't, I don't know that you don't wear it? That you can pass? That sounds awful I know, but you don't get put into a box, you're free to be whatever you want without people making judgments before they even know you. You have an advantage in a way. People can be awful to brown people. I know.

SALT BABY:　Were you awful? Did you have opinions about brown people?

ALLIGATOR: No! Of course not. But I mean Christ, some of the shit I've heard my family say, it's fucking sick.

SALT BABY: Well they are going to love me.

ALLIGATOR: They will love you.

SALT BABY: Because I don't wear it? Because I'm not so brown? Because they can pretend that I'm Portuguese or something? I don't have to be the Indian at the table I can be ambiguously ethnic. What a privilege to be me eh? I get to be whatever I want, whatever I want except the one thing I am.

ALLIGATOR: All I'm saying is that you get to choose, you have a choice.

SALT BABY: I don't want the choice I just wanna be browner. *(Beat.)* I don't even tan well. I get all blotchy.

ALLIGATOR: You don't need to be browner to be Indian. I'm allowed to say Indian now right?

SALT BABY: Let me run it by the band office.

ALLIGATOR: I think you're perfect. Blotchy tan and all.

SALT BABY: Yeah?

ALLIGATOR: Absolutely.

                    Time shift. ALLIGATOR and SALT BABY are out front of ALLIGATOR's parents' house.

ALLIGATOR: You nervous?

SALT BABY: Should I be?

ALLIGATOR: No. Not really.

SALT BABY: Not really?

ALLIGATOR: No, not at all.

SALT BABY: You seem nervous, you wanna back out?

ALLIGATOR: No. No we can't I think they've already seen us.

SALT BABY: Well that's comforting.

ALLIGATOR: It's going to be fine. *(He grabs her face and looks her in the eye.)* It will be fine.

SALT BABY: OK now you're freaking me out.

ALLIGATOR: It will be fine. *(More for himself.)*

SALT BABY: It will be fine. You wanna know why? 'Cause I brought this. *(She pulls out a magnum of chardonnay.)*

ALLIGATOR: Mom is going to love you.

SALT BABY: I know right? Ready?

ALLIGATOR: I think so.

                    Shift to dinner.

                    SALT BABY, ALLIGATOR and his parents are in mid prayer. ALLIGATOR is making a blow job gesture to SALT BABY, she gives him the finger and is busted by ALLIGATOR's dad, TERRY.

CHERYL: …let us thank you for this food. Amen.

TERRY: Amen.

CHERYL: *(Finishing her glass of wine.)* Thanks again for the wine, but you really didn't have to do that.

TERRY: Yeah, you really shouldn't have.

CHERYL: *(Gives TERRY cut eye, turns back to SALT BABY.)* So where did you say you are from?

SALT BABY: Um, Six Nations. Six Nations Reserve. Near Brantford.

CHERYL: Oh. Oh yeah… *(She tops up her glass.)* So that means you are…you're…

TERRY: Indian, Cheryl, that's the word you're looking for.

CHERYL: Terry! You don't say Indian anymore! I'm sorry—

ALLIGATOR: Christ. Five minutes in, you guys have set a new record.

TERRY: Oh relax.

ALLIGATOR: Don't patronize me.

TERRY: Calm down.

CHERYL: Can we just have a nice dinner, please? *(Turning to SALT BABY.)* More wine?

TERRY: Jesus, Cheryl, not everyone can drink as much as you. She's barely eaten anything. Not that I blame her…

CHERYL: No one is forcing you to eat anything here. Why don't you just go over to your girlfriend's house and eat whatever she cooks you!

TERRY: Not this again. We work together Cheryl, that's it. We work together. Someone needs to pay the bills.

CHERYL: I work Terry. I work.

TERRY: Avon Cheryl? Really?

ALLIGATOR: Could you guys not? Please?

CHERYL: It's hard work. I'd like to see you try.

TERRY: Sit on my ass all day and play dress up with old ladies for a living? No thanks.

CHERYL: Why do you insist on belittling me in front of company?

TERRY: I think you do a fine job of that yourself. More wine dear?

ALLIGATOR: Seriously guys? Please.

Silence.

SALT BABY: Thanks so much for having me. This is really good.

CHERYL: *(Stifled crying.)* You'll have to excuse me I have a terrible migraine all of a sudden. *(She exits.)*

TERRY: Christ. Excuse me. *(He follows CHERYL.)* Cheryl.

ALLIGATOR: Fuck I am so sorry. They haven't been like this in a while I thought…

SALT BABY: It's fine.

ALLIGATOR: No it's not. They are awful. I shouldn't have brought you. I'm sorry.

SALT BABY: It's fine. Really. Are you OK?

ALLIGATOR: Just supremely embarrassed.

SALT BABY: Hey don't worry. Everyone's family is fucked up in their own way. I just got them on a bad day.

ALLIGATOR: Yeah. *(Pours more wine for himself, offers some to her she declines.)*

SALT BABY: I'll drive.

ALLIGATOR: Good. Cause I think I need to forget that that just happened. *(Big drink.)*

SALT BABY: *(She goes to him, holds him.)* It's fine. I promise I'll still sleep with you.

ALLIGATOR: Yeah?

SALT BABY: Uh huh. I might think about your dad while we're doing it though, he's kinda hot.

ALLIGATOR: Well it's good you think that, I may look like him one day. Come on let's get out of here before they come back.

He picks up the wine. They exit.

SALT BABY stands at a check out. WANDA B, the clerk, struggles to understand tax exemption forms.

WANDA B: Sorry about this. So I take off the…?

SALT BABY: PST.

WANDA B: OK so if I can just see your card. OK. And I write down…this number?

SALT BABY: I'd just write down both.

WANDA B: Good idea. OK. And you sign here.

SALT BABY signs the form.

Don't worry it isn't a treaty or anything. (*She laughs.*)

SALT BABY: What?

WANDA B: Sorry bad joke.

SALT BABY: Yeah…

WANDA B: You know, Native people and signing papers…

SALT BABY: Yeah I got that.

WANDA B: Hey, I'm Native too. Well part.

SALT BABY: Oh yeah, which part?

WANDA B: Ha. Yeah. No seriously. I just found out my grandmother was part Cherokee.

SALT BABY: Cherokee eh?

WANDA B: Yeah. So can I ask you something?

SALT BABY: Sure.

WANDA B: Well how Native are you? Like are you full? You're not full right?

SALT BABY: No I'm not. I'm just over half.

WANDA B: Oh. 'Cause you don't really, you know, look it.

SALT BABY: Guess that all depends on what you think Native people look like right?

WANDA B: Can you tell? That I am? Can you see it?

SALT BABY: I don't know, I mean maybe.

WANDA B: No huh?

SALT BABY: Uh…

WANDA B: Well it's just nice to meet someone who doesn't look it you know? Makes me feel like I make a little more sense. So how do I get one of these? *(She holds up status card.)* 'Cause I really want to buy this new flat screen and this would really help.

SALT BABY: I don't know. I don't think you can.

WANDA B: Oh. Why?

SALT BABY: You'd have to go through the government. Maybe you could I'm really not sure.

WANDA B: I should totally try. *(She examines the card.)*

SALT BABY: Can I have my stuff now?

WANDA B: Oh yeah sure. *(Hands bag and card to SALT BABY.)* Here you go.

SALT BABY: OK then. Bye.

WANDA B: Bye. *(Does an awkward 'how' Indian pose.)*

On the Rez. SALT BABY drags ALLIGATOR toward DAD's home. They pause at the front door.

SALT BABY: It will be fine.

ALLIGATOR: I doubt it will be fine. You don't know what it's like to meet the father of the girl. 'Cause the dad, the dad knows and he wants to kill you but he can't or he hasn't been given the chance. And your dad has guns!

SALT BABY: Just calm down. It'll be fine. It can't be as bad as meeting your parents.

ALLIGATOR: That's true.

SALT BABY: My dad will probably say "hey nice to meet you," and then he'll take off to his room to watch UFC.

ALLIGATOR: UFC? He watches UFC? Christ, why is your dad so violent?

SALT BABY: Oh stop. God you are such a pussy. Come on.

                    They enter the house.

               Hello? *(Beat.)* Dad?

                    DAD enters quickly with bloody hands.

ALLIGATOR: Oh god! *(He hides behind SALT BABY.)*

DAD: Hey.

SALT BABY: Hey. *(They hug avoiding his hands.)* Dad this is Al.

DAD: Hey Al. I'd shake your hand but I don't think you'd enjoy it very much. You caught me cutting up my deer.

ALLIGATOR: Yeah. No. Sure. Of course. Nice to meet you sir.

SALT BABY: How many points?

DAD: Eight.

SALT BABY: Nice.

ALLIGATOR: Is it alright if I use the bathroom?

DAD: Sure it's just outside there down the trail to the left.
               Watch out for the wild dogs.

ALLIGATOR: What?

SALT BABY: He's kidding. Just kidding. It's up at the top of the
               stairs.

ALLIGATOR: *(Tries to enjoy the joke.)* Ha yeah. I'll be right back.

               They watch him leave.

SALT BABY: You totally did that on purpose.

DAD: Oh come on that was hilarious. Did you see his
               face? He's kinda scrawny.

SALT BABY: I like 'em scrawny.

DAD: I don't need to hear about that.

SALT BABY: You'll like him once you get to know him. He's
               funny.

DAD: Funny eh?

SALT BABY: Yeah.

DAD: Does that make up for him being scrawny?

SALT BABY: Stop he's gonna hear you. Be nice. He's never been
               on a Rez before. He's already petrified.

               ALLIGATOR returns.

DAD: Hey Al, you wanna see my latest harvest?

ALLIGATOR: What, like corn?

SALT BABY: Not exactly.

               *Transition to the garage, there is a deer gutted and
               hanging.*

ALLIGATOR: Oh my god.

DAD: Nice one eh?

ALLIGATOR: To be honest sir I have no idea.

SALT BABY: What are you gonna do with it?

DAD: Dunno. Still deciding.

SALT BABY: Pepperoni's always good.

DAD: What do you think Al, pepperoni?

                 ALLIGATOR tries to stop her.

SALT BABY: He's a vegetarian.

DAD: Oh.

ALLIGATOR: You know, health reasons. I don't even like it…

DAD: Sure. Well. I'm about to go watch my show. Big fight
              tonight.

SALT BABY: Oh yeah?

DAD: You watch UFC, Al?

ALLIGATOR: Uh no, not too much.

DAD: If you change your mind. (*He exits.*)

ALLIGATOR: That went well.

SALT BABY: It was fine.

ALLIGATOR: He thinks I'm a girl.

SALT BABY: You kinda are. Come on. I'll make you a salad or
              something. (*She begins to exit.*)

ALLIGATOR: Hold on. (*He pulls a toothbrush out of his pocket.*)

SALT BABY: Uh huh. That's nice.

ALLIGATOR: No, you don't understand, it's your dad's.

SALT BABY: Eww. What the fuck? That's a bit creepy. What are
             you doing with my dad's toothbrush you freak?

ALLIGATOR: DNA. Your dad's DNA is all over this. You could
             take the test now. I grabbed it when I went to the
             bathroom.

SALT BABY: What the fuck?

ALLIGATOR: You can take the test. No more online past life tests
             and psychics and all that bullshit. He never needs
             to know.

SALT BABY: I can't do that. That's—that's really wrong.

ALLIGATOR: Just take it. And then you have the option.

SALT BABY: No. That's…I don't need to know like that.

ALLIGATOR: Just take it. Or at least think about it.

SALT BABY: Would you put that away? What if my dad comes
             out and sees you waving his toothbrush around?
             Way to make a first impression. Just…here give it
             to me. (She takes it.)

ALLIGATOR: It's up to you.

             She looks at the brush.

             Shift.

             The DNA kit arrives.

             SALT BABY and ALLIGATOR in their apartment.
             She holds the kit deep in thought.

ALLIGATOR: I appreciate you doing my laundry, I do. I just wish
             you would check the pockets. This is the second
             time you have washed my wallet. You're not a
             domestic. I get that. Just don't worry about it I can
             do my own laundry. OK?

She does not respond.

So did you wanna go out for dinner?

No response.

Or we could stay in.

Nothing.

Are you pissed?

Nothing.

Hello?

Nothing.

Hey. *(Beat.)* HEY!

SALT BABY: Sorry. *(Beat.)* What?

ALLIGATOR: Where the hell were you?

SALT BABY: I'm just thinking that…I don't know, maybe I don't
               want to take the test.

ALLIGATOR: You ordered the kit, paid for it and now you don't
               want to know?

SALT BABY: I should just take my family's word for it. They say
               "we are" so "we are" should be enough. And my
               dad is so against it.

ALLIGATOR: He's just afraid you'll find out you're 50%
               milkman.

SALT BABY: Oh fuck you.

ALLIGATOR: Then don't take it. So did you wanna go out?

SALT BABY: I just think if I ever had kids I'd want—

ALLIGATOR: Whoa! Kids? Hold up.

SALT BABY: Who said they'd be with you? You can put the captain away. I don't need your baby batter.

ALLIGATOR: What's wrong with my batter?

SALT BABY: Nothing. It's just that...well...it's just that you're, you know, you're white.

ALLIGATOR: So?

SALT BABY: Well you know there's a lot of pressure on me to have a brown baby. And they are the cutest, white kids are kinda hideous.

ALLIGATOR: So let me get this straight, you won't have a kid with me, or any other white person, because there's pressure on you to have a brown baby and because white kids are ugly.

SALT BABY: In a nutshell yes.

ALLIGATOR: Who the fuck are you? That is beyond fucked, you realize that right?

SALT BABY: If I have kids I want them to be Indian. I do.

ALLIGATOR: And they will be Indian. If you are their mother then they will be Indian. That's the way it works.

SALT BABY: But if I have kids with a white person then that will weaken my kids blood quantum. They will have weak Indian blood.

ALLIGATOR: You don't even know how much Indian blood you have. You could be Dutch or some shit and you've already decided that you need to have Indian kids?

SALT BABY: Try and think about it from my perspective. The pressure on me to "keep the blood." People have actually told me that the future is in my womb. I know what it sounds like, I do. Fuck I didn't know you had some deep desire to be my baby daddy.

ALLIGATOR: It's not that and you know it.

SALT BABY: Then what is it?

ALLIGATOR: We will only ever go so far in this before you being Indian trumps everything else and we'll have to end it.

SALT BABY: I don't know. Who says I even need to have kids? The world is too fucked anyway right?

ALLIGATOR: Right.

SALT BABY: Hey I didn't think you wanted kids?

ALLIGATOR: I just didn't know I didn't have the choice.

SALT BABY: Look, this isn't something that either of us wants right now so why even talk about it? Let's just forget it OK?

ALLIGATOR: Yeah, sure.

ELDER and SALT BABY sit preparing for ceremony.

ELDER: Is there anything you'd like to put in the centre?

SALT BABY: Uh no. I didn't know I had to sorry. I can go get something.

ELDER: It's not necessary, I was just asking. Relax, this isn't church, you know?

SALT BABY: Sorry I've never been to one of these before, I'm kinda nervous.

ELDER: There isn't anything to be afraid of, just relax. You come to this with an open heart and a clear mind. You haven't drank in the last four days right?

SALT BABY: No I haven't.

ELDER: Good. No drinking or any of the green stuff *(Pot smoking gesture.)* for four days after, right?

SALT BABY: Right. Can I ask you something?

ELDER: That's why I'm here.

SALT BABY: Why does this shit scare me? Sorry not this shit, but
              this stuff, this traditional stuff it really freaks me
              out. There are things that click and make sense but
              there are other things that I just don't know about.
              Like the rules and why so many? And who made
              them up you know? I get the preservation factor,
              like we need to establish these things so they don't
              disappear, but sometimes it feels like every other
              institution I don't agree with. I want this to be right
              I really do. It just feels so stuck, so stagnant. And
              why do I feel like such and asshole when I say these
              things? What the hell kinda Indian am I?

ELDER: You need to find out what works for you. This path
              may not be your path. It doesn't make you good or
              bad.

SALT BABY: It's hard not to feel that way sometimes, bad you
              know? Like a bad Indian.

ELDER: Bad Indian?

SALT BABY: 'Cause I don't know much. I feel like I should know
              more than I do.

ELDER: What do you know?

SALT BABY: About this stuff?

              ELDER nods.

              I've been to Longhouse a few times mostly for
              funerals and Sunday breakfast. But that never
              really, clicked for me.

ELDER: What clicks for you?

SALT BABY: Sweetgrass. Sweetgrass has always felt right to
              me.

ELDER: That's mostly a man's medicine.

SALT BABY: I know. But I grew up with it. It was always around
                and I didn't even know that it was a man's medicine
                until I got older. I guess cause my Dad raised me
                and that's just what we used.

ELDER: What did he teach you?

SALT BABY: It was a long time ago.

                DAD enters. In memory.

DAD: When I was just young I had this friend and we
                used to play down by the dam. We'd make boats
                outta garbage and sticks, whatever we could find,
                then we'd race them, see who could get their boat
                over the dam first. This one day we were racing
                them and this boy he got real mad cause my boat
                kept beating his boat, so he starting cheating. He
                was pushing his boat with a stick trying to get it
                ahead of mine, but he pushed it too far and he fell
                in. At first I laughed cause he was cheating and so
                I thought he deserved it. But then he didn't come
                back up. I waited and waited. Undertow pulled
                him under and that was it. The river just swallowed
                him up.

                (Holds a braid of sweetgrass.) Here.

SALT BABY: What do I do?

DAD: Hold it and let the smoke go over you. Like this.
                *(He bathes in the smoke, closes his eyes and brushes the
                smoke over his eyes.)* So you see clearly. *(He brushes the
                smoke over his ears.)* So you hear honestly. *(He brushes
                the smoke over his heart.)* So you feel truthfully. *(He
                hands the braid to her.)*

SALT BABY: What if I do it wrong?

DAD: You can't do it wrong. There is no wrong. This is
                between you and the creator.

SALT BABY: It's just feels scary.

DAD: Because it is powerful and it's old. Older than anything. *(He hands her the braid.)*

SALT BABY: *(She repeats the motion of ears, eyes, heart.)* Was that OK?

DAD: How do you feel?

SALT BABY: Good.

DAD: You don't have to be scared of this. It is yours as much as it is anyone else's. Don't forget that.

SALT BABY: So if we do this why don't we ever go to Longhouse or anything?

DAD: Well if you wanna I'll take you. I just don't like all the rules. Never liked the rules.

SALT BABY: How come?

DAD: Just felt too forced for me. I say pray however you wanna and just try and be nice. Respect those before you and those coming after you.

SALT BABY: Those coming after?

DAD: The ones who aren't here yet. This is theirs too. We need to respect that.

SALT BABY: So you probably shouldn't have put garbage in the river then huh?

DAD: No probably not.

ELDER: Your dad sounds pretty smart.

SALT BABY: Yeah he is.

                        The apartment. ALLIGATOR is playing video games.

ALLIGATOR: Come on, come on. AW YOU WHORE!

> *SALT BABY enters. ALLIGATOR's attention is divided between the game and SALT BABY.*

ALLIGATOR: Hey.

SALT BABY: Hey.

ALLIGATOR: How was it? AW FUCKER!

SALT BABY: It was fine.

ALLIGATOR: Helpful?

SALT BABY: I don't know. In the end I didn't do the ceremony. I just felt weird about it. I have too many questions.

ALLIGATOR: Come on, come on. BITCH!

> *SALT BABY sits.*

So does that mean we can go for a drink now? Four days before and after is off now, right?

SALT BABY: Wow. That's great. You are just so supportive and just so fucking helpful.

> *He pauses the game.*

ALLIGATOR: What? It's just a question.

SALT BABY: You can do whatever you want I'm staying in.

ALLIGATOR: Oh no you don't. If I go out now it seems like everything is fine and then I get home and this shit—this shit starts—

SALT BABY: This shit? This shit? Does it seem like everything is fine? Does it really seem like I am fine? It is not fine. I just really don't see how you could help.

ALLIGATOR: Blame whitey time.

SALT BABY: What? Fuck you! You put that on me that 'whitey' bullshit.

ALLIGATOR: I do? *(Under his breath.)* You've got to be fucking kidding me.

SALT BABY: You know I'm right here, you can stop shit talking me under your breath, I'm right fucking here.

ALLIGATOR: No. No you are not right fucking here, you haven't been here for a long time.

SALT BABY: What?

ALLIGATOR: You. You are constantly, I don't know, vacant or something.

SALT BABY: Vacant? Jesus grow a pair.

ALLIGATOR: You know what, forget it. I'm going out. This isn't going anywhere and I don't feel like doing this with you tonight.

SALT BABY: You're right this really isn't going anywhere. It really isn't at all.

ALLIGATOR: So what are you saying?

            Silence.

            No, go ahead, say it.

SALT BABY: You just don't get it. I don't know if this could ever really work. You'll always be...I don't know, confused about things, about me.

ALLIGATOR: Jesus. I'm in no way confused about you. You are confused about you. I know you. You need to figure you out.

            He begins to leave.

            Let me know when you're feeling Indian enough to be with me.

            He exits.

SALT BABY alone, new apartment. She listens to sad bastard music. Unpacks things. GRANDPA enters. He picks up a book she unpacks.

GRANDPA: What the hell is tah-fu?

SALT BABY: Tofu. It's gross. Not my book.

GRANDPA: Didn't work out with the bag of bones huh?

SALT BABY: Nope.

GRANDPA: New place?

SALT BABY: Yep.

GRANDPA: It's nice.

SALT BABY: No it's not. *(She breaks down, he goes to her.)*

GRANDPA: Hey, hey, hey. It's OK, it's going to be OK.

SALT BABY: I should have known. Clara warned me it wouldn't work, that it couldn't work.

GRANDPA: Ah don't listen to her.

SALT BABY: She was right. I should have known. I was a leather jacket, an exotic fruit.

GRANDPA: Your gonna listen to a lady who saves bread tabs and buttons in her basement?

SALT BABY: Not just her the psychic too. She said, she asked me if I was leaving a relationship.

GRANDPA: She also told you you were an armadillo.

SALT BABY: She was right about some stuff. I should have thought about it.

GRANDPA: She smelled like dirt.

SALT BABY: And his parents hated me.

GRANDPA: They didn't hate you they hated each other.

SALT BABY: I should be with an Indian guy. I should.

GRANDPA: You really think so?

SALT BABY: I think it will be easier.

GRANDPA: Then quit moping around. Look at you you've been living out of boxes for a month now. Never gonna meet anyone like this. You gotta get out there.

SALT BABY: I don't know if I'm ready for that.

GRANDPA: Never gonna know until you try.

> *PHILIP sits at a table in SALT BABY and ALLIGATOR's bar/café. SALT BABY enters and approaches PHILIP.*

SALT BABY: Hey. Hi…I'm sorry are you…?

PHILIP: Philip? Yes. Hey.

SALT BABY: Hey sorry I'm late. You know Indian time. Ha. Yeah. So. I've never done anything like this, you know one of these things.

PHILIP: A date?

SALT BABY: HA! No, I've been on dates before. Just not like this you know.

PHILIP: I'll try and keep it as painless as possible.

SALT BABY: I am so not starting off well.

PHILIP: Why don't you sit down and we can start there.

SALT BABY: Sure. Yes. Right.

PHILIP: How are you?

SALT BABY: Good. Pretty good. Yourself?

PHILIP: Good. So your profile said that you're Mohawk?

SALT BABY: Yep. From Six Nations, my mom's Mohawk, dad's Tuscarora.

PHILIP: Oh.

SALT BABY: You're Mohawk right?

PHILIP: Yeah.

SALT BABY: Cool.

PHILIP: Yeah. So this place seems…nice.

SALT BABY: Yeah. They've got pretty good food. I used to come here all the time, not so much anymore. You hungry?

PHILIP: I'm OK.

SALT BABY: Sure. So your profile says that you hunt?

PHILIP: Yeah, deer and turkey mostly.

SALT BABY: My dad hunts.

PHILIP: Oh yeah? Bow?

SALT BABY: Mostly rifle.

PHILIP: Oh. *(His phone rings. The ring tone is Pow Wow music.)* Sorry. *(Looks at phone, annoyed.)* Just one second.

SALT BABY: No, sure go ahead.

PHILIP: Hello. No. No, I can't talk right now. Just drop him off at my mom's and I'll pick him up there. My mom will look after him until I get there. I'm not doing this with you right now. I'll call you later alright? Alright? OK. Bye. *(Hangs up.)* Sorry.

SALT BABY: Everything OK?

PHILIP: Yeah, it's fine.

SALT BABY: You sure?

PHILIP: Yeah it's fine. So how'd you end up on Rez-Fox-dot-com?

SALT BABY: Well I've been wanting to meet more Indian guys and this just seemed like the easiest way.

PHILIP: Indian guys?

SALT BABY: Yeah, it's hard to meet Indian guys in the city, so I've dated a lot of white guys.

PHILIP: A lot of white guys?

SALT BABY: Well not a lot of white guys, I'm not a whore or anything.

PHILIP: OK.

SALT BABY: I've been trying to meet a nice Indian boy for a while.

PHILIP: You know when you use the word "Indian" you are doing a disservice to yourself and our entire race.

SALT BABY: Oh shit sorry. I didn't mean to offend you.

PHILIP: We are Haudenosaunee, people of the Longhouse. (Pronounced ho-den-oh-Show-nay.)

                 GRANDPA enters.

SALT BABY: Oh. Yeah. I'm just not used to, you know saying that to people.

PHILIP: When you speak of us like that it gives the white man power over us.

GRANDPA: This guy seems like an asshole.

SALT BABY: I know.

PHILIP: Do you go to Long House?

GRANDPA: Oh Christ.

SALT BABY: Not in a while.

PHILIP: You should.

GRANDPA: I think you might be cousins.

SALT BABY: What? Why?

PHILIP: It's important for us to keep the traditional way
                of life alive. I can introduce you to some people if
                you'd like.

GRANDPA: He kinda looks like you.

SALT BABY: I don't think so.

PHILIP: Oh. OK.

                Silence.

SALT BABY: So…

GRANDPA: Well this is uncomfortable.

PHILIP: I'm just going to go to the bathroom.

SALT BABY: Yeah.

                PHILIP exits. Beat.

GRANDPA: He's not coming back is he?

SALT BABY: Nope.

GRANDPA: Ah, he was a jerk anyway. Hey isn't that the bag of
                bones?

SALT BABY: Oh god. *(She briefly panics, fixes herself.)*

                *She approaches ALLIGATOR. GRANDPA watches
                from a distance.*

                Hey.

ALLIGATOR: Holy shit hey.

SALT BABY: Still got the mouth of a sailor I see.

ALLIGATOR: Hey as I remember you weren't a fucking saint.

SALT BABY: *(Laughs.)* Nice.

ALLIGATOR: So how have you been? What's new?

SALT BABY: Are we actually going to have this cliché of a conversation? The "how-have-you-been-what's-new-conversation?" Let me guess, now I say, "You look good," and nod my head and smile.

ALLIGATOR: And a montage of our relationship plays in our heads with a bittersweet sound track?

SALT BABY: And then for a brief second we contemplate doing it again?

ALLIGATOR: We were good at it.

SALT BABY: Yes we were.

ALLIGATOR: Remember that time in the movie theatre?

SALT BABY: Which time? Remember when that old lady caught us? God that was bad.

ALLIGATOR: No that was good. Really good. Slut.

SALT BABY: Oh fuck you. You loved it.

ALLIGATOR: Yes I did.

                    Silence.

SALT BABY: Hey I still have a few of your books. Vegetarian cookbooks and a couple of CD's. Must've gotten mixed up with my stuff in the move. You could stop by and pick them up, or I could meet you somewhere, you know if you wanted them. Or whatever.

ALLIGATOR: Well, I'm not missing them so you keep them or just get rid of them if you don't want them.

SALT BABY: Sure. Yeah that's fine. Well I should go.

ALLIGATOR: Yeah me too. It was good to see you.

SALT BABY: Yeah. See you around.

ALLIGATOR: Yeah.

> *Ex-lover hug. They begin to exit.*

Hey.

SALT BABY: Yeah?

ALLIGATOR: Did you ever take that DNA test?

SALT BABY: Uh, yeah.

ALLIGATOR: You did? Really?

SALT BABY: Yep.

ALLIGATOR: No you didn't.

SALT BABY: Yes I did.

ALLIGATOR: Liar.

SALT BABY: I did.

> *ALLIGATOR examines her face.*

ALLIGATOR: I can tell when you're lying.

SALT BABY: No you can't. I took the test, I did. You wanna know the results?

ALLIGATOR: Not really, no.

SALT BABY: No?

ALLIGATOR: Nope. It was really good to see you.

SALT BABY: Yeah you too.

> *GRANDPA walks to her. They watch him go.*

GRANDPA: He wasn't so bad eh?

SALT BABY: No, he wasn't.

GRANDPA: How come you lied? About taking that test?

SALT BABY: I don't know. I guess I just wanted to see.

SALT BABY watching TV alone. She is disheveled. It is early in the morning and she has been up all night.

TV HOST: Welcome to the show RJ. Now are you ready to find out if you are in fact little Twileesha's father?

MALE GUEST: I'm ready for the truth! The truth!

TV HOST: Alright. Well, here it is. The truth RJ. When it comes to the paternity of little Twileesha…you…are…the father!

Audience hoots, hollers etc.

FEMALE
GUEST: I told you! Didn't I tell you! I told you!

DAD enters.

DAD: Jesus. What in the hell are you watching?

SALT BABY: Something about men taking care of their own.

DAD: Does it gotta be so damn loud?

SALT BABY: I guess not.

She turns off the TV. DAD sits beside her.

DAD: So, how long you staying?

SALT BABY: Don't know. Why you wanna get rid of me?

DAD: Heck no. You know I wish you'd move home. Get out of the damn city.

SALT BABY: I know.

DAD: So how are things with what's-his-head?

SALT BABY: What's his head? It's done. Over.

DAD: Oh?

SALT BABY: Yeah, well it wasn't ever going to work anyway. Waste of time.

DAD: Why do you say that?

SALT BABY: 'Cause he's white.

DAD: You broke up with him because he's white? Jeez. You didn't tell him that did you?

SALT BABY: Well yeah. He wanted to know so I told him.

DAD: You dumped his scrawny ass 'cause he's white?

SALT BABY: Well…yeah…

DAD: Really?

SALT BABY: Mostly.

DAD: Were you happy? Did he make you happy?

SALT BABY: Doesn't matter now, he hates me. Thinks I'm crazy, thinks I'm some sorta AIM Indian.

DAD: You sorta are.

SALT BABY: Ha ha. (Beat.) I think I screwed this up.

DAD: I don't know.

SALT BABY: Think I did.

DAD: It wasn't right. The time wasn't right for you to be with him. One day it will be right.

SALT BABY: Just not with him.

DAD: No not with him. Can I ask you something?

SALT BABY: Yeah.

DAD: Would it make a difference?

SALT BABY: What?

DAD: That DNA stuff. Say you knew it all, all the numbers and percentages. Would it really change anything?

SALT BABY: It doesn't matter. Look do we have to do this now? I'm trying to watch this. (*She goes to turn on the TV.*)

DAD: Hey, what's going on with you?

SALT BABY: Nothing. I'm just tired OK? (*She lies back down.*)

DAD: Hey. You don't wanna talk that's fine but don't get mad at me.

       She sits up.

SALT BABY: I'm not mad. Just— Look you don't want to know. You didn't want to give me the sample. Fine. I get it. You're scared you'll find out you're Dutch or something. It's fine.

       Silence.

DAD: OK.

SALT BABY: What?

DAD: I'll do it. Sign me up or whatever you have to do. Get your kit. Take my blood. This isn't enough for you. This place, these people, me, we aren't enough for you. You need more, more than I can give you. You need answers from some lab far away. Whatever I say, whatever I tell you it'll never be enough.

SALT BABY: Dad I need—

DAD: You know when you were little you got sick really sick and I was scared. So scared. Doctors didn't think you would make it. One night you were doing real bad.

                GRANDPA enters. SALT BABY is aware of him, DAD is not.

                You had a high fever and your Grandpa, he came up to me in the hospital and he said…

GRANDPA/
DAD: Don't you worry. She'll make it. She's a tough one.

DAD: He called you—

GRANDPA/
DAD: *Chic-heh Oo-t'goh-threh.* (Pronounced Chick heh oo gooth ray.)

DAD: He said it meant—

GRANDPA/
DAD: Salt Baby—

DAD: —in Tuscarora. And that you were a fighter and you always would be. He said that there was strength in that name he said—

GRANDPA/
DAD: —she's a scrapper,

GRANDPA: —probably your Mohawk side.

DAD: He said that—

GRANDPA: —you were gonna have to be tough. That—

GRANDPA/
DAD: —it wouldn't be easy

DAD: but you could do it. And he was right, you did, you pulled through. But you did have to fight, not just then in the hospital but all the time. I remember this one time when you came home from school and you had been in a fight cause someone called you white. I was mad at you for fighting but you were madder. Took you all night to calm down. You were just riled up. And now, I look at you here like this and I wonder if you still are that person. If you still have that fight in you. I wonder where that strength went. This life is hard. I know that better than anyone. But you have family, and a history that runs through you. If you need to do this, if you need me to do this, then I will.

GRANDPA and DAD look to her.

SALT BABY: You know I used to hate my hands. I always thought they looked manly, wide nails, short, stubby fingers. I wanted different hands so badly. But when Grandpa died I remember at the funeral looking down at his hands, crossed in front of him and I realized I had his hands. And I was so happy to have a part of him with me forever.

I don't need to do this. I don't need you to do this. I know. I've never not known. I just forgot I knew. I'm sorry.

They hug.

GRANDPA/
DAD: Hey—

DAD: It's OK.

GRANDPA: Do something for me?

DAD: You want some pancakes?

SALT BABY: Sure.

DAD begins to leave.

GRANDPA: Shake your Dad's hand for me?

SALT BABY: Dad?

DAD: Yeah?

SALT BABY: I'm supposed to give you this. *(She holds out her hand.)*

> *DAD looks. A moment. He shakes. They exit.*

> *The End.*

Grandma Betty's Indian Cookies

4 cups of flour

2 tsp baking powder

2 tsp baking soda

1 tsp salt

1 tsp nutmeg

1 cup of butter

2 cups of brown sugar

1 cup of sour cream or buttermilk

1 tsp vanilla

2 eggs

Preheat oven to 375 degrees F.

Combine dry ingredients and set aside.

Cream butter and sugar together, then add eggs. Add sour cream (or buttermilk).

Combine wet and dry ingredients.

Roll out onto a lightly floured surface. Use a cup of biscuit cutter to cut cookies out.

Place on a baking sheet and bake for 10 minutes.